Chicken Soup for the Soul.

Love That's Meant To Be

Amy Newmark

CSS

Chicken Soup for the Soul, LLC
Cos Cob, CT

Chicken Soup for the Soul: Love That's Meant To Be
Amy Newmark

Published by Chicken Soup for the Soul, LLC www.chickensoup.com
Copyright © 2019 by Chicken Soup for the Soul, LLC. All Rights Reserved.

The publisher gratefully acknowledges the many publishers and individuals who granted Chicken Soup for the Soul permission to reprint the cited material.

Front cover photo courtesy of iStockphoto.com/martinedoucet (©martinedoucet)
Interior photo of penguins courtesy of iStockphoto.com/jtstewartphoto (©jtstewartphoto)
Photo of Amy Newmark courtesy of Susan Morrow at SwickPix

Cover and Interior by Daniel Zaccari

ISBN: 978-1-61159-712-7

PRINTED IN THE UNITED STATES OF AMERICA
on acid∞free paper

25 24 23 22 21 20   03 04 05 06 07 08 09 10 11

Table of Contents

Kismet

*Love at first sight is easy to understand; it's
when two people have been looking at each
other for a lifetime that it becomes a miracle.*
~Amy Bloom

I hadn't wanted to attend the wedding that night, and I discovered later that he hadn't been keen on it either. I would have rather gone to my friends' annual Ugly Sweater Christmas Party with my closest and rowdiest friends than get dolled up and make small talk with people I didn't know. I barely knew the groom; I had yet to meet the bride; and the last thing I wanted to do was pretend to recognize fellow guests as my mom presented them to me.

Don't get me wrong, I am in no way anti-social or a Scrooge. Quite the opposite, actually. It was two weeks before Christmas, and I was head-to-toe, inside-and-out, chockfull of holiday spirit, which meant Christmas music, Christmas movies, Christmas cookies, Christmas sweaters, and Christmas parties. I didn't want to miss a single candy cane, ornament exchange, or verse of "Rudolph the Red-Nosed Reindeer" the entire month of December.

But when your mother asks you to be her date at a wedding, you go. It's not a debate. There's no question about it. You just go. So, off I went to the wedding where I would know seven people — including my mom and myself. I eased into the car, careful not to slip on the ice or fall into the foot-and-a-half of snow that had blanketed Chicago earlier that week. There I was, in my black-and-silver dress, an elegant overcoat that in no way kept me warm, my curls pulled into a loose up-do, and my feet shoved into Jewel bags and then into my black, fuzzy winter boots. What can I say? I'm a classy chick.

I gazed out the frosted car window, listening to Brenda Lee singing about how she was rockin' around the Christmas tree and imagining my friends doing just that. I had hoped that my mom and I could bail after dinner so I could still make it for most of the party, but we were carpooling with my mom's friends, so I was on their time. No telling what that could mean. I was lost in thought, imagining the warmth of my friends' basement, decorated with multicolored Christmas lights and garland, the TV playing *A Christmas Story* in the background, and everyone standing around laughing and noshing on chili and artichoke dips, pizza, and homemade cookies and cakes, when I heard my mom say, "… so maybe you'll like him. We'll see."

Her words shook me from my reverie. "Like who?" I asked. "Are you talking to me?"

My mom was fiddling in her purse in search of gum as she repeated, "An old friend of mine… She and her husband are going to be at the wedding, and they want to introduce you to their son."

"Mom!" I gasped. If I hadn't wanted to go to the wedding before, this made me want to leap from the moving car.

"Oh, relax," she said, popping a piece of Trident in her mouth. "Just say hello. You don't have to do anything you don't want to do."

That wasn't the point. I hated being put in situations like that. My mom knew it. My friends knew it. Everyone who knew me knew it. Lately, however, it seemed like people were trying harder than ever to find me the "perfect guy."

About four years earlier, my decade-long relationship with my first and only boyfriend came to an overdue end, and I hadn't dated, in the conventional sense, since. Not a boyfriend. Not a real date. Not even a friend-with-benefits in nearly four years, and apparently everyone but me found this worrisome.

The funny thing was, I was actually happy being single. I know, I know... single people often say that to mask the fact that they haven't found the right person. And everyone around them rolls their eyes.

But the truth of the matter is that I really *did* feel that way. I spent twelve years with the same person, and I needed time now to just be me.

There was a lot I needed to learn about myself and what it meant to be fully independent and self-reliant, so that's what I did for the four years following my break-up. I learned. I traveled. My social calendar was jam-packed, and not just on weekends. I had something going on every night of the week. And despite the fact that I was always exhausted, I loved every minute of it. I took advantage of every opportunity life afforded me. I said "no" to nothing — except dating. And this drove my friends crazy.

When we entered the reception hall a half-hour later, that couple and their son happened to be among the first guests we encountered. Luckily for me, he was extremely shy and didn't so much as look up when his mother introduced us. I nodded hello and, when he looked down, I took the opportunity to make a beeline for the coat check.

My mom knew so many people there; so I followed her around the room as she kissed and hugged everyone, and it turned out that I knew more people than I anticipated. But that didn't stop me from checking my phone every so often to see how quickly time might be passing. We all moved toward the back of the ballroom where the ceremony took place, and once it was over, we found our seats near the bar.

My mom and I had been seated with people we didn't know, and that isn't necessarily a bad thing if the people are friendly; however, this group seemed like they intended to talk amongst themselves. Suddenly, we heard someone calling my mom's name from the table beside ours.

"Maria! Maria!"

We turned to see a petite blonde in a tight, black dress waving us over.

"We have two empty seats," she said in Spanish. "The couple isn't coming. Why don't you and your daughter sit with us?"

Mom took the seat beside her friend, and I took the only remaining seat left, next to a handsome guy who appeared to be around my age. Even seated, it was clear that he was tall with a medium build and, in my opinion, resembled soccer great Leo Messi, but even better looking. I noticed a stunning, svelte blonde seated beside him, whom I assumed was his girlfriend, so I didn't bother making conversation. I surveyed the ballroom, admiring the Christmas lights and decorations, listening to bits and pieces of conversations, mainly in Spanish since most of the guests were from Argentina, and every so often, stealing a glance at "Leo."

As I was buttering my bread, my mom made eye contact with him and said in English, "Hi, I'm Maria. And you are?"

He smiled and said, "Pero yo soy Argentino." *But I am Argentine.*

They shook hands, smiled, and a look of recognition suddenly crossed my mother's face.

"Sos el hijo de Donato y Lourdes?" she asked.

Are you Donato and Lourdes' son?

"Si," he replied. "Soy Marcos." *Yes, I'm Marcos.*

"No lo puedo creer! Como esta tu mami?" she asked. *I can't believe it. How is your mom?*

And with that, Marcos moved the centerpiece to reveal his mother sitting beside the svelte blonde. My mom and Lourdes exchanged hugs and hellos, and soon our table was bubbling with conversation, laughter, and reminiscing. I soon learned that Luz, the blonde seated next to Marcos, was simply a good friend of his, and so I felt more comfortable conversing with him. I was captivated by his charming Argentine accent as well as the way he spoke with confidence and honesty. We talked throughout dinner, and I realized that, for the first time in years, I had met a guy with whom I didn't want to stop talking. We could've sat there all night, and I would have been content.

At one point, Luz asked Marcos if he wanted to go outside and have a cigarette, and he replied, "No, I'm okay right now."

He turned back to me.

"You don't smoke?" I asked him.

"No, I do," he said, "but I want to stay here and talk to you. Is that okay?"

My heart leapt. I couldn't remember the last time I felt that way. Happy. Calm. Enchanted. And, most important, not afraid or hesitant. It was the strangest feeling, but it felt as if I had come home. Something about him was so familiar, so comforting. I had known him for only a couple of hours, but I felt at ease, as though my heart had found its beat.

We spent much of the evening talking and flirting. At the end of the night, he came up to the bar where I was chatting with old friends to say goodbye. The music was blaring, so as he leaned in to speak in my ear, all I heard was "your number."

"You want my number?" I asked him, smiling.

"No," he said. "I have your number. Maybe we could have dinner sometime."

I wrinkled my brows, confused. I was fairly certain I hadn't given out my phone number that evening.

"I didn't give you my number," I said.

"I know," he said. "Your mom did."

Leave it to my mom. She knows me better than I know myself.

On the car ride home that evening, I said to her, "Mom, I have a feeling that Marcos is going to be a significant part of my life. I don't know why, but something tells me that I have not seen the last of him."

Two years later, during that same pre-Christmas week, Marcos and I married.

Throughout our courtship, we came to learn that our paths had crossed long before we were born. Our families are from a small town in southern Italy called Ripacandida, and our grandfathers knew each other well. Eventually, they immigrated to Buenos Aires, Argentina. Marcos' grandfather was a tailor, and he made the suit that my grandfather wore when he married my grandmother.

In the early 1980s, Marcos' parents decided to move to Chicago, and Marcos was born in the hospital where I was born. We were even delivered by the same obstetrician. His family lived here for approximately four years before returning to Argentina, and during that time, my grandparents and parents shared a friendship with Marcos' parents — so much so that Marcos and his brother called my grandmother "Nonna" (Grandma in Italian).

Our families were overjoyed when Marcos and I started dating. Just before we got engaged, his father visited us from Argentina, and he brought with him a photograph of us when we were little. We were on a carousel at a neighborhood carnival. I was three at the time, and Marcos' brother was four, and we sat side-by-side on horses with my dad standing between us. Only eighteen months old at the time, Marcos was sitting on a horse behind his brother as his mom propped him up. Currently, that photograph is tacked to our refrigerator, and I often look at it in amazement. Who would have thought that, thirty years earlier, I was sharing a carousel ride with the man who would be my husband?

Fate is a funny thing. A beautifully funny thing. Just a few short years ago, I was desperately trying to get out of going to a wedding where I would meet my future husband, the man my heart had been seeking. I believe that Marcos and I were truly made for each other, that our souls had been searching for each other throughout our lives. Our history is proof of that.

On our wedding day, as we recited our vows to each other in English and Spanish, I remember thinking to myself, *This is where I was always meant to be. All the ups and downs, the questions, the doubts, were leading me down the path to this moment and this man. My husband.* He was already a part of my history, my blood, and my story, woven into the fabric of my life.

Never did I imagine on that frigid winter night,

while my friends were sipping eggnog and drunkenly singing Christmas carols, that my soul would find its mate — and my life would be forever changed.

— Vanessa Angone-Pompa —

Bollywood Dreams

Our soul mate is the one who
makes life come to life.
~Richard Bach

They meet, break out in choreographed dance with beautiful music, and fall in love. Then the movie ends, and we turn off the TV. That's love in the world of Bollywood.

Growing up in America in an immigrant family, I was in love with my Indian culture. I helped my mom cook, watched Bollywood movies like it was my job, and even danced and performed traditional

Indian folk dances.

One day, I knew, I would marry my "Bollywood Princess." I had posters of Kareena Kapoor on my walls, and when I hit my early twenties, my family started introducing me to potential brides to meet from the arranged-marriage system of aunties, who were excited to play matchmaker. The plan was to marry the perfect bride: a great cook, beautiful, with a love for family. Of course, she would be Indian. And not only Indian, but from Gujarat, the state our family is from. And not only Gujarati, but also a Patel—and ideally a specific Patel from these five villages my family comes from. Simple, right?

But it didn't happen. By my late twenties, I had written two books and was traveling as a speaker and trainer. More books were written, and soon I was called to speak around the world. Instead of flying back and forth to home for a couple days, I decided to live on the road full-time as a nomad. Traveling made my heart soar. My family was happy about my success, and yet very concerned.

"Jaymin, when are you going to settle down and get married?"

"No one will want to marry you if you keep traveling everywhere! Get a job in one city where you can start your family."

For nearly a decade, I had happily met the women my family members set me up with. I "courted" here and there, but no relationship lasted. It was the same story each time. She wanted me to settle down, and my soul wanted to travel. It felt like I must live my passion *or* find love and start my own family. I just didn't see why I would have to give up what I loved doing to have a family. I was ready to give up hope. I was slowly coming to terms with the idea that perhaps my exciting, purpose-filled life would be spent alone.

Then, one weekend, I was invited to speak in Seattle. A friend had been trying for years to introduce me to a woman who lived there, but geography had never been on our side. I reached out, and we carved out a couple hours to connect with each other.

In that short time, we learned we had grown up with many similarities and interests. We had attended grad school to get our MBAs the very same years. We had even attended some of the same conferences without knowing it! We graduated with nice corporate jobs, which we then quit to travel around the world. Eventually, we became coaches and speakers because we wanted to help others with our life's work. It was like meeting the female version of me!

More importantly, I couldn't forget how she made me feel. She had this amazing presence and warmth that invited me to show up fully and authentically. She was gentle, curious, open and accepting. In those few short hours I spent with her, I felt so safe and seen. It was a magical feeling.

Soon after, we found ourselves speaking in San Francisco at the same time. We made plans to connect. What was supposed to be a lunch date on Sunday became lunch and dinner on Sunday, exploring the city on Monday, supporting each other's speaking events on Tuesday, enjoying a lovely picnic on Wednesday, and postponing my Thursday flight so we could also spend Friday together.

That evening, after one of her workshops, she took me in her arms and asked, "Do you want to be my partner?"

Partner? I was stunned. I wanted to say yes, but this wasn't happening like my Bollywood dream. She was so amazing, but she wasn't a Patel from the five villages, she wasn't Gujarati, and she wasn't even Indian! She was a mix of Polish and Swedish heritage, with bold blue eyes and curly blond hair. There was no way my family would accept me marrying her, so why date her? But the feelings from spending the entire week together could not be denied, and I followed the voice in my heart and said, "Yes!"

Six weeks later, we were back in Seattle brushing our teeth, and it hit me. I turned to her and said, "Just so you know, I'm going to marry you. How long do I have to wait before I ask?"

Her eyes flashed a smile, and being a relationship coach, she said, "Well, we are currently enjoying 'new relationship energy,' so I would say it's too soon right now. You'll have to wait at least six months."

I nodded, smiled, and kept brushing my teeth.

After what felt like the longest six months, we were engaged. What was supposed to be one lunch date had turned into a week, and had now turned into a lifetime. My friends couldn't believe it — I was finally going to get married! My family was less excited by my actions. They were hugely disappointed that I didn't choose a wife from those five small villages in Gujarat as they had expected me to do.

I had taken a bold step. It was not the Bollywood dream I had imagined, but I listened to my heart and knew it was the right decision.

My wife is the most amazing person I've ever met. She is medicine and magic. She has taught me that people do not *fall* in love; they *rise* in love. Anything feels possible with her.

Together, we are raising two children as we travel

the world full-time as nomads. We have published a total of nine books, and continue to coach and speak everywhere we visit, sharing our story and our message to inspire others. It's a bold move, and not always an easy one. We face the same issues that all parents face — no sleep at night, sickness, bumps and bruises and crying, in addition to scheduling problems and travel upsets as we move to a new home every few weeks. But it's all worth it. I learned that I can, in fact, have it all. I just needed to follow my heart and say "yes" to the moment.

I was always told life was about making tough choices. I never felt like I could have it all. Finally, through meeting the woman of my dreams, I've proved the old adage wrong. You can have it all.

I did have my Bollywood love story. We met, we fell in love, and now we're dancing in sync to the beautiful music of life's ups and downs together.

—Jaymin J. Patel—

The Face in the Window

A dream you dream alone is only a dream.
A dream you dream together is reality.
~John Lennon

I was divorced, thirty-four, with a beautiful son, when I first attempted to decipher the chaos of my many dreams. Surely, there must be messages there or something my subconscious was attempting to convey. At that time, I was not involved in a relationship, and I certainly had no wish for another failed marriage. I hadn't even dated for a couple of years and concentrated only on meeting the needs of my child and clearing my head of old, muddled thinking. Even so, I was open and interested in meeting a man of honesty and honor.

Then came the night of *the* dream — a dream so piercingly clear that it would alter the course of my life.

In this dream, I was engaged to marry a young sailor, complete with sailor cap, navy shirt, white pants and a neatly trimmed beard. The year was sometime in the 1940s. The place was Pearl Harbor, Oahu, Hawaii. The sailor's name was Johnny, and he was on a short leave for his birthday. I had made a birthday cake and decorated the dining area with brightly colored strips of crepe paper and balloons.

When he walked into the small bungalow and came directly over to me, I stretched out my arm, which came to rest on his. I could feel every single hair on his arm right down to the texture and the downy feeling of the hairs. The sailor spoke not a single word; he merely stared into my eyes with bold, fierce strength. I could feel the sense of his love wash over me and I knew that this man loved me truly and without question. The message was undeniable.

Just as quickly as it had begun, the dream was over. But the lasting effects of that dream stayed with me, day in and day out. I wrote down every detail that occurred in the dream, every movement, every emotion. It felt so very real, and I knew this dream held profound secrets for me. As to the secrets, I knew nothing. I only knew that the sailor, Johnny, loved me, and that felt as real as any moment in my life had ever been.

Days and weeks passed, and I found that I looked for Johnny's face and his sailor cap in crowds wherever I was — at the grocery store, the mall, social gatherings. I felt a strong need to find him. I also felt I might be losing my mind — looking for a person from my dream was ludicrous. One day, I became certain I was losing my grip on reality. I stood at my kitchen sink and looked over to a nearby sliding glass door — and saw Johnny's face in the reflection of the glass. It was plain as day — the face, the beard, the sailor cap — it was all there.

The following day, Johnny's image reappeared in the same location. That night, I saw his reflection in my bedroom window. He was seemingly following me as the days and nights flowed into weeks and then months of seeing Johnny's face nearly anyplace I traveled. I was absolutely certain I had lost my mind, but decided to put this to a test. On a business trip, I joined a co-worker in Oregon to help her coordinate a surgical convention. On our last day, we enjoyed a wonderful lunch along the coastline. Johnny's face appeared in the window as we gazed out over the beautiful beach scene. Finally, I asked my co-worker if she saw anything unusual in the window glass. She said no, she'd seen nothing out of the ordinary. I was devastated and certain I was indeed insane and had lost my mind. I cried and grieved for days.

Finally, I confessed everything to my best friend, whom I had positioned to stand at my kitchen sink and look over to the sliding glass door. However, she saw absolutely nothing. With this, I decided that I needed professional help, and I scheduled an appointment with a psychiatrist.

A group of friends was planning to gather at my apartment once a week for several weeks for numerology classes presented by a psychic whom I had come to know and appreciate. I was looking forward to having good friends around me to share some happy times and ease my worries. One of these friends brought along another friend, a girl named Sherry, whom I had never met. Sherry was a bright and cheery soul. When they first entered my apartment, she came right over to me as I prepared food items at my kitchen sink. She put an arm around my shoulder, introduced herself, and then grinned like crazy and asked, "Who's the sailor dude in the window?"

I nearly fainted. *Did I hear Sherry correctly?* I had. She went on to say that she clearly saw a dark-haired, bearded man with a sailor cap, and this image had been reflected in the glass of my sliding door. I nearly wept right on the spot, but kept my emotions under control throughout the remainder of the evening. The following morning, I canceled the appointment with the psychiatrist. Although I could not explain the image appearing in glass, the message was crystal clear. The man from my dreams was following me and making certain his image was kept fresh in my mind.

Life returned to normal, or what felt nearly like normal. One of my friends and co-workers attempted to set me up with a blind date, but I continued to say "no" for many weeks. Finally, I relented. Larry, I was told, was newly divorced and eager to meet me. My friend's husband knew him quite well and vouched for his character.

Soon, the night of the blind date arrived. When I opened my front door, I was not prepared for the sight before me. Without question, the man was identical to Johnny — right down to the hair, the beard, and the stature — but without the sailor cap! I was completely stunned.

The blind date continued at the seafood restaurant Larry had chosen. Once seated, we began to talk and shared many things from our childhoods. It turned out that Larry had wanted to be a sailor and always wore a sailor's cap until his mother finally took it away from him at age seven! I confessed that I had wanted to be a professional dancer, and although I had been given a full scholarship to a dance academy in San Francisco, I was unable to attend as my family moved soon after to another state.

Back at my apartment, Larry and I talked endlessly. He mentioned a childhood friend he always dreamed of — a little blond girl who always wore a two-piece, short red outfit and always had the smell of old shoes around her. That set me to thinking, and I brought out an old photo album filled with some pictures from my childhood. When Larry browsed through the pages, he stopped abruptly on one and said, "This looks just like the girl from my dreams — the girl with the red outfit."

The picture was black and white, but he was correct: My short, little outfit was indeed red! And as my father owned a shoe-repair store at that time, the smell of old shoes permeated those years of my life. Larry could not have known these things, but somehow he did.

We talked until we heard the birds chirping at dawn. We both felt like we had known each other before from another life, and perhaps we had. I now believed that anything was possible.

Eight days later, Larry got down on one knee and proposed. We were married soon after in a small wedding ceremony on Orcas Island in the San Juan Islands off Washington State. The witness, who was unknown to us, sat down at the piano and played a beautiful Hawaiian wedding song, which reminded me that my dream had been set on Oahu.

The man of my dreams had become real, and we shared a real love. It felt exactly like the love emanating from the sailor in my original dream.

Larry and I were married for twenty-eight years before his death.

Dreams really do come true.

— Louetta Jensen —

I Almost Gave Up on Romance

*First romance, first love, is something so
special to all of us, both emotionally and
physically, that it touches our lives and
enriches them forever.*
~Rosemary Roger

It had been five years since my last real date.
The post-divorce rebound taught me to be
cautious, and looking online left me feeling
empty, so I tried not to want a man in my
life. Maybe I was better off single. Maybe the dogs,
my most loyal companions, would be enough.

In January 2011, I promised myself I wouldn't

look anymore, at least until my daughter graduated from high school in June.

Six months after I made that promise, on the Tuesday night after my daughter's graduation, I sat down at the computer in the hallway alcove. It had been another long day at work. My hands ached, and my eyes wanted to close as I scanned my in-box and then diverted to Facebook, hoping to relax.

A private message was waiting for me. I clicked the icon and stared at the name for several seconds as my weariness evaporated. My heart pounded as I read the message: *Greetings to you! After many years, I hope you are well. Take care and be safe!*

I looked at the name again, and then sat back from the computer. Could it really be him? My first love in high school? I took a deep breath. Maybe I was seeing things.

Like a skeptical jeweler studying a diamond, I moved closer and read the name again. I'd typed that name into the computer a few times, but gave up after seeing how many people had the same name as my first love. And besides, I was the one who wrote to him last in 1972, so it was his turn. Now, in 2011, he was finally getting back to me with this simple message that made my heart feel like it was going to leap out of my chest.

David was a good guy when we dated in high school, but so much time had gone by. A person can change a lot in thirty-nine years. But the timing was too much to ignore.

Wow! It's so nice to get your message! I typed, and then added a little about sweet memories and high-school friends. I sent him a friend request, figuring he was still far away. If he turned out to be a jerk, I could simply unfriend him.

As we progressed from Facebook to phone calls, David didn't sound like a jerk at all. He sounded very interesting. He worked as a firefighter/EMT in Connecticut, and he had three dogs. He talked about his dogs like they were family. Beep, his ten-year-old Australian Shepherd mix, couldn't climb the stairs anymore.

"Yep, I carry the old girl upstairs to the bedroom every night," David told me.

My heart wanted to melt, and my toes tingled at the image of him carrying his old dog upstairs at bedtime. "Must love dogs" had been on the top of my list, the one I made in case I ever decided to take a chance on love again. As David and I talked on the phone, a tiny ember of hope — almost forgotten after so many years — glowed in my heart.

Still, I kept reminding myself to stay grounded, to keep my ears open and my brain fully engaged. I asked a lot of questions, and he didn't mind answering them. "Nothing's off the table," he told me.

One night, David had a question of his own. He asked me what I was doing on Friday, July 15th. He said he had some time off that weekend and wanted to take me out to dinner. I was hesitant. Talking on the phone was one thing, but…

"Are you still there?" he asked.

"You want to come all the way from Connecticut to North Carolina just to have dinner with me?"

"Yep, with one catch."

"What's the catch?" I tried to sound businesslike.

"I'd like to spend time with you on Saturday, to sit and talk, to find out what has brought you to this point in your life."

I had to take the chance. I agreed. It was a date.

And a wonderful date it was! We ate dinner at a cozy restaurant near the river. As David talked about his career and the lessons he had learned, I realized he had become a man of integrity. After dinner, we walked along the riverfront, and then sat on a bench to watch the golden sunset. I leaned back against him and let his strong arms hold me gently. The natural scent of his skin, which must have imprinted itself on my teenaged brain, was intoxicating. His kiss awakened feelings I had not felt in a long time.

David was a perfect gentleman on our first date, and on all the dates thereafter. He flew down from Connecticut about once a month, and I flew up to meet his friends and family, including the dogs.

We talked on the phone every night between visits, asking questions, giving honest answers, and sharing our hopes and dreams.

On December 9th, three days before my birthday, David joined me on a church outing to Brookgreen Gardens in South Carolina. After dinner, we strolled under the live oaks lining the walkway. Twinkling lights and luminaries transformed the gardens into a land of magic as musicians played holiday melodies on flutes and violins.

We meandered to a path less traveled near the back corner of the gardens where white globes on poles stood like giant lollipops.

"What do you want your future to look like?" David asked.

"I want you to be in my future," I smiled, wondering what he might have in mind.

"I want you in my future, too," he said.

We stopped to gaze at the moon, and then David turned to face me. I looked up into his blue-grey eyes and noticed the moonlight gleaming silver on his hair.

"Will you marry me?"

"Yes," I answered without hesitation, and then added on impulse, "but you have to get down on one knee."

"Do you want me to ask you again?"

"Yes."

He looked around. No one was watching except the moon. David granted my request and asked again, "Will you marry me?"

"Yes!" I laughed. "Of course, I will!"

One year later, after I'd almost given up on romance, I married my first love, my last love, the love of my life.

— JoAnne Macco —

Random Certainty

Do you think the universe fights for souls to be
together? Some things are too strange
and strong to be coincidences.
~Emery Allen

I met him the evening before the second semester of my junior year in college. I had seen him the night before at tryouts for the drama department's spring production. When the director introduced him as a sixty-hour major with professional experience, I remember whispering to a friend, "Sigmund Bonebrake… that's got to be his stage name. Nobody could have a name like that."

Even though his acting was excellent, he looked

so young, like a fourteen-year-old. It did not seem plausible that he could have much experience. He was an enigma.

I met him the next evening in the Den at the Student Union. When the students he was sitting with left, a friend of mine brought him to my table. Don introduced us and promptly left as well. I began chatting with him tentatively, a bit shy at having to entertain someone I didn't know. I began by asking him how he liked the school so far and what he thought of tryouts. When I found myself more at ease, I asked him to tell me more about himself. He told me he had spent four years in the Army, attended three colleges for a brief time, worked in Kansas City as a cab driver and a printer, and lived in Australia for two years where he was part of a trapeze act in a carnival and was in a couple of movies. Looking across the table at him, I found his story difficult to believe. After all, he looked barely old enough to drive.

I was skeptical, but when I questioned the veracity

of it all, telling him he couldn't have done all that since he was too young, he grinned and pulled out his driver's license. I was shocked into silence as I saw he was not fourteen, but almost thirty. In order to break the awkward silence, I suggested we go bowling at the lanes adjacent to the Den. Later, he walked me back to my dorm.

As classes began, I found that Sig was in four of mine, and he managed to find a seat next to me in each one. I actually began to believe he was as old as he claimed because he had impeccable manners. He carried my books, opened doors for me, and pulled out my chair at tables — all behaviors most boys my age had never learned or practiced.

We became almost inseparable. We had breakfast together in the college cafeteria, took our classes together, and met in the Den for suppers before rehearsals where we worked lights and sound together. During quiet times, we learned about each other, our likes and dislikes, past adventures and mis-adventures, and hopes and dreams for the future.

Then, one day, I discovered two bits of information about him that I felt were signs that our relationship was meant to happen. The first sign was that one of the productions Sig had been involved in during his fifteen years in theater had won a competition that had been broadcast on national television. Remarkably, I remembered seeing that broadcast and even specifically remembered his portrayal of the character in that production. I remembered explaining to my sister that they must have used a trampoline to accomplish the spectacular jumps his character had made.

The second sign we were meant to meet revealed itself when we were sharing our love for writing poetry. I told him I had been published in a book of Iowa poetry three years earlier, and I was eager to show him my poem. He told me that he had also been published in two subsequent issues of that same publication. While he returned to his dorm to get his copies of the books, I retrieved my copy to show him. I read his poems first and was amazed at their beauty and complexity. When he wanted to read mine, I found I was almost embarrassed to show him my simple poem. But I let him read it, and he was most complimentary.

Then he said, "I think I'm published in this issue as well."

"No," I replied. "I read this issue cover to cover when I got it, and I'm sure you aren't. There aren't any poems by a Sigmund Bonebrake in this book. I would certainly have remembered that name."

He flipped through the book slowly, looked at me, and then smiled. "Yes," he said. "Since I was in Kansas City at that time, my aunt in Iowa published one of my poems under her name."

And then he showed me his poem. As I read it, my heart stopped. Of all the poems in that entire edition, his poem had been my favorite.

Two weeks later, when he asked me to marry him, I thought again of those signs — and I said,

"Yes." Thanks to random certainty, we'll be celebrating our fiftieth anniversary soon.

—Sue Bonebrake—

Ooh La La

*Romance is the glamour which turns the dust
of everyday life into a golden haze.
~Elinor Glyn*

O*oh la la — how romantic these Italians
are!* That was my thought as I watched
a carload of Italian construction
workers disembark at my hometown
train station in France.

World War II had just ended, and Europe was in
the midst of rebuilding itself. It was a monumental
task that moved a lot of skilled craftsmen throughout
the various countries.

After a wartime period when most men were
off fighting, it was a joy and a relief to finally have

them back. First, the good-looking American soldiers came through, liberating France in the process. Then the builders arrived, often romantic Italians with bedroom eyes. It was almost too much for a gal to handle.

I was a young French woman at the time, working at a factory job all day, while helping out at home in the evenings. All my earnings went toward helping with the family's household expenses. In order to purchase anything extra for myself, I worked extra hours on weekends, harvesting crops in the fields or doing other odd jobs. It was a tough, hardscrabble life, but we were young and could manage.

As a result of my heavy work schedule, contact with others came in the brief moments between jobs, as I bicycled from one workplace to another. When I zipped home in the evenings, I would see groups of other workers who were also getting off work. Among them, the dark-haired Italians would stand out, chatting between themselves as they were taking in their unfamiliar surroundings.

From time to time, I'd see a particularly attractive Italian fellow who caught my eye. I was still pretty naïve, so I didn't really know how to get his attention. My flirting skills left much to be desired. I knew that the construction workers moved from town to town, repairing and rebuilding as needed. So I had a limited amount of time to figure out how to get noticed by this lad.

Daydreaming of this handsome Italian filled my workdays, as I imagined what my conversations with him would be like once I got to know him. I couldn't wait for the end of the day when I could whiz by on my bike to my next assignment and hopefully catch sight of him. Snatching the odd glimpse of him kept me going through long months of hard work.

Finally, there came the time when I didn't see him around anymore. As I had feared, his job probably ended in our area, and he was on to the next place, most likely never knowing I even existed. I was dejected and inconsolable. This faux romance had kept me going for so long.

Time passed, but I never forgot about my ideal Italian man. It seemed absurd, but I felt I truly loved him from afar. I swore I would never forget him, and I did not want to befriend anyone else to take his place. I constantly kicked myself for not being bolder while I had the chance.

My father tried to console me, saying there were plenty of fish in the sea. Like countless others, he also worked in construction, so he knew many single young men were out there looking for love. In fact, he said, a very nice Italian guy was working on his crew. He would bring him home for dinner one night.

I didn't want to know about any other Italians, nor did I want to cook a special dinner for an unwanted guest. I had enough work to do. I was looking for fun and love, and I had just lost my greatest opportunity.

Nevertheless, against my wishes, my father

arranged a date to bring home his young work colleague. I made sure to make a plain, unappetizing meal, hoping to dissuade my father from ever doing it again. It was my form of passive-aggressive protest.

On the evening of the dinner, I stayed in my factory work clothes, refusing to dress up for company. It was bad enough that I was stuck making dinner for everyone in the family, plus an unwelcome guest. I didn't want to expend any more energy than I had to.

Finally, my father and his young worker arrived on their bicycles and came in the door. You can imagine my surprise when I found myself face-to-face with the very same Italian I had been swooning over for the better part of a year.

Dinner and the rest of the evening were a blur. The young man seemed truly appreciative of a home-cooked meal and being amongst a family, despite my earlier efforts to make things less than hospitable. We finally managed to break the ice that evening and get to know each other a little.

It was the beginning of a romantic love affair that lasted a lifetime.

—Denise Del Bianco—

One in 300,000

*He stirred my soul in the most subtle way and
the story between us wrote itself.*
~Nikki Rowe

A quick slap from my best friend, Christine, caught me off-guard. "What was that for?"

"He's leaving." She bobbed her head a few times in his direction. I peered over her shoulder and saw the man she was referring to, phone to his ear, lingering near the garden exit.

I pursed my lips and gave her a shrug. "Maybe it's just not meant to be."

"You have to talk to him!"

I gave him another glance. He was handsome. I

crossed my arms and slowly tapped my foot at her. "He didn't talk to me. And besides, if it's meant to be, I'll see him again."

She shot me her sweet look of disapproval. I gave her one back and turned to resume my stroll through the gardens. It wasn't long before I heard her little heels clicking behind me.

"Dar, this is the third time you've run into him. In a city of thousands and thousands of people. Three. Times." She waved her three little fingers in my face as if I couldn't hear her.

My cheeks flushed. She had a point. "Oh, yeah, I can see it now. He looks like he's with his parents. 'Mom. Dad. This is Darla… We met in a bar….'"

She squared her hands on her hips. "We are grown-ups, for God's sake. And it wasn't a bar. The first time was a restaurant."

I nodded. I remembered it clearly. It was a restaurant — Primanti Bros. in Market Square. I ran inside that night to take cover from the rain. My co-workers and I had ventured to the square for happy hour as we did most Friday nights in the summer, but we were met with a sudden downpour. All of us, dripping wet, squished into the area in front of the registers. That was when my slightly intoxicated co-worker got a little too silly telling a story and hit a young man in the back of the head. He turned, and our eyes met. I promptly pointed to my friend, Lori, but being seven years her senior, I still felt slightly responsible and apologized for her behavior.

He smiled with his hazel eyes. "It happens." And then he handed me his phone. "It's John. Can you talk to him while I order?"

Before I knew it, the phone was in my hand, and the man turned back to the server where he continued to place his order. I chatted with John for a few minutes, at which point I found out the man whose cell phone I held was named Chris.

As quickly as it started, the rain stopped. Chris thanked me, took back his phone, and resumed his conversation. My friends and I went on our merry way.

"Dar?"

I shook off my thoughts and turned back to Christine. "Sorry. Yes. It was a restaurant, but the second time was definitely a bar."

"Yeah. And you never did get his number."

"That was your fault," I reminded her. We both laughed.

She and I continued to wander through the gardens. We were there to hear live jazz, not chase men. But I couldn't help thinking of that second time I saw him. Christine and I had accepted a ride from the guy she was dating. He took us to the Boardwalk on the north side of town, where nightclubs and bars were lined up along the river. Christine wandered off with her date as I lingered near the bar. I felt a tap on my shoulder and turned to see the man with hazel eyes. It had been three weeks since our Primanti's encounter, and I honestly could not place him. He could tell.

"You don't remember me, do you?"

I bit at my lower lip and shook my head. Nothing.

"Primanti Bros. A couple weeks ago. Your friend smacked me in the head."

"Oh… right."

We laughed and made small talk the best we could, but the people and the noise cut short our conversation.

There was something about him I liked, though. His eyes focused solely on me. He had an air of confidence, but wasn't pushy. His dark hair complemented his tan skin.

"Can I get your number?" he asked after a while.

"How about I take yours?" I countered.

He patted his pockets and chest. No pen. No paper. "I'll be back. Wait here?"

"Sure."

No sooner did Chris slip off into the crowd when Christine grabbed me. "We have to go. Our ride!" she yelled while pointing toward the exit.

"Hold on." I looked in every direction, trying to see over and through the crowd. The man with the dark hair and hazel eyes was nowhere to be found.

"Now!" she demanded again. "Our ride!"

I followed Christine and her date into the night, figuring if it was meant to be it would somehow happen.

Christine and I spent the rest of our day in the gardens unhurried and unworried about the man known as Chris. I never did talk to him that day. And he left without saying a word to me. That day marked seven weeks since I had run into him the first time, but we still had not exchanged last names or phone numbers. That encounter was number three in a city of 300,000 people, and now he was gone... probably forever.

I took that as a sign that we weren't meant to be.

That is, until about two weeks later...

I had returned yet again to Market Square with my co-workers. This particular Friday was special as one of the younger guys in our group was turning twenty-one. I congratulated my friend and offered to buy him a drink. He accepted, and so we headed into the 1902 Tavern. We wound our way through the many people in the entrance, trying to make our way to the bar. And then I saw that man with hazel eyes and dark hair, standing directly in front of me at the bar.

I stopped dead in my tracks. Speechless.

He smiled. "Are you stalking me?"

"Me? Are you sure it's not the other way around?"

To make a long story short, my friend got his birthday drink. As for Chris and me, we left the bar and spent the rest of the evening sitting in the window seat of a local coffee shop chatting the night away. It's been seventeen years now that we've been married, and we have four precious children. As we navigate the ups and downs of marriage, I always remind myself that we were meant to be together. What other explanation could there be for running into the same person four times in three months in a city of 300,000 people?

— Darla S. Grieco —

Long Odds

*Accept the things to which fate binds you, and
love the people with whom fate brings you
together, but do so with all your heart.*
~Marcus Aurelius

In the spring of 1989, I was, like almost
everyone else in the world, glued to my
television set, watching the astonishing
events unfolding in a large public square in
the heart of Beijing called Tiananmen. I had a personal interest in China, for I was about to embark
on a new career as a college teacher in Xinjiang
Province. But after June fourth, when Chinese
troops moved on Tiananmen Square to disperse
the students, killing hundreds possibly thousands

of people (we will never know the exact number), my Canadian sponsor phoned to tell me that, due to political uncertainty in China, the contract had been cancelled. Broke and disheartened, I moved into my mother's basement and found work as a costumed interpreter in a museum run by Parks Canada.

But as the saying goes: When one door closes, another opens. As it happened, my supervisor at the museum was on maternity leave, and the supervisor from Bethune Memorial House, another national historic site, had been asked to fill in temporarily. One day, this acting superintendent walked into the lunchroom with a fax in his hand and asked half-jokingly if anyone would like to go to China and teach English. "It seems that the Bethune International Peace Hospital is looking for an English language instructor. Anyone interested?" This fortunate coincidence came about because the Canadian surgeon Dr. Norman Bethune had served with the Communist Eighth Route Army during World War II and had established the first front line mobile army surgical hospital.

So it came to pass that in a few weeks, I found myself in Shijiazhuang, a grimy, industrial city of over a million people located some 280 kilometres south of Beijing, standing in front of a class of doctors and nurses, teaching conversational English.

The China I experienced was not like China today. This was old-style Communist China — perhaps more so because the events in Tiananmen Square had prompted a conservative backlash. Foreigners were only permitted to stay in government-approved accommodations. The hospital, because it had an international connection with Bethune, often had foreign guests, so it had a special hostel within the walled grounds for foreign visitors with its own segregated dining room where we had to eat all of our meals. My movements were very restricted. I was not allowed to visit Chinese homes without permission from the local police bureau. There were no private telephones or private cars. All news sources were vetted by government censors, and this was long before cell phones and the Internet could circumvent such control.

In the room next to mine in the government-approved hostel lived another Canadian named Nancy, who taught English at a nearby medical college. Because of the restrictions on our movements, we ate every meal together in the hostel's dining room and spent all of our free time in each other's company. This might have been a recipe for disaster if we proved incompatible, but we hit it off right away. We felt immediately at ease, as if we'd known each other all our lives.

Before we knew it, our Chinese minders — khaki-clad romantics all — were matchmaking. They set up chaperoned dates, dance parties with our students, and cultural visits to the few local historical sites that had survived the ravages of the Cultural Revolution. Our contracts only overlapped by a month, but I promised to get in touch with Nancy once I returned to Canada. Today, she is my wife of more than twenty years, and we have three lovely children.

Consider this: If the protest in Tiananmen Square had not happened, then my contract in Xinjiang would not have been cancelled. If I had not been working in the museum on that particular day, and if my supervisor had not been on maternity leave, I would never have heard about the job at the Bethune Hospital. And if I'd had the freedom to choose my own accommodation once I arrived in China, I might never have met my future wife. My children would never have been born.

Yet if our freedom is less perfect than we suppose, we are still faced with choices. The students in Tiananmen Square could have chosen complacency, but instead they chose to speak out against entrenched corruption. And given the opportunity, I still had to choose to go to China. It is a decision I will never regret.

— Hugh Kent —

Hey, Ma, I Called that Girl from the TV!

*I knew the second I met you that there was
something about you I needed. Turns out it
wasn't something about you at all.
It was just you.*
~Jamie McGuire, A Beautiful Wedding

kay, so let me admit up front that the above is a somewhat misleading title. I never really said that to my mother (and even if I did, I would *never* have used the expression, "from the TV!"). But it *is* true that the first time I laid eyes on the

woman who would become my wife was when she appeared on my television set… and it was on my *birthday* no less!

It was October 18, 1985, and it was indeed my twenty-ninth birthday. But I was in no mood to celebrate that Friday night after what had been an exhausting and frustrating week at the brokerage firm where I worked. I just felt like zoning out in front of the boob tube and watching my "guilty pleasure" TV series, *Dallas*. Normally, I'd be checking out *Wall Street Week* on PBS just prior to it, at 8:30, but after the week I'd had, the last thing I wanted to hear about was the stock market.

I grabbed the remote and started flipping from channel to channel… until I came upon a friendly, familiar face. It was legendary music promoter, Sid Bernstein — the guy best known for bringing The Beatles to America. I had actually met with Sid about eighteen months earlier when I was managing a talented young singer. Apparently, he was now the host of this TV variety show here in New York. I decided to watch.

I seem to recall the first act on the show being a one-armed Chinese accordion player (although my wife, to this day, swears it was mega-hit songwriter Alan Gordon). Then Sid introduced a "bright new musical talent" whom he said he had just met earlier that day—Miss Dana Britten. I remember watching her sing and thinking, *She's kinda cute, and the melody is really catchy. But the lyrics kinda suck. I could definitely help that chick in that area.* After the girl finished singing, Sid spent a few minutes chatting with her.

Sid: "So tell me, Dana, what's going on in your music career these days?"

Dana: "Honestly, not much, Sid. Some stuff is brewing, but who knows if it'll actually work out."

I certainly was not used to hearing that kind of refreshing candor from an aspiring music artist. I liked her. I wrote the young lady's name on a short list I kept of promising young singers/actors/actresses to "keep an eye on."

Well, two months later, Sid had this Dana Britten chick appear on his show again. And then, in early April 1986, she was a guest for the third time. She sang another original song and chatted delightfully with Sid afterward. I remember thinking to myself that night, *Hmm… maybe I'll try and catch her if she's playing around town.*

It was the very next evening that I was in a car riding home from a concert. My date was driving, and we had on WABC radio. The interviewer, Alan Colmes, was talking to singer/songwriter, Rupert Holmes. A young woman caller asked Rupert about some obscure songs he had written for The Partridge Family. In my head, I was thinking, *This girl is as weird as I am with the music trivia stuff!* And her voice, for some reason, sounded strangely familiar. Then, as she was about to hang up, I heard Alan Colmes say, "Hey, thanks for calling, Dana."

And that, my friends, was the moment I absolutely *knew* that I had to call Dana. The synchronicity of the events leading up to this moment was too obvious to ignore. So that Monday, I decided to phone Sid Bernstein. And he actually took my call.

Me: "Hey, Sid. I don't know if you remember me from our meeting a while back…"

Sid: "Oh, yes, Gary. I do remember you. How can I help you?"

Me: "Sid, I've really enjoyed that Dana Britten you've had on the show a few times."

Sid: "Oh, yes, she's a sweetheart!"

Me: "I'd love to see if she'd be interested in some co-writing. But her phone number is unlisted. Do you happen to have it by any chance?"

Without hesitation, Sid gave me Dana's unlisted home phone number. And that night, I left the following message on her machine: "Hi, Dana. My name's Gary Stein. Sid Bernstein gave me your number. If you want to hear a really interesting story, give me a call at 212-517 — ." Later that evening, Dana did return my call.

"I cannot believe Sid gave out my personal phone number to a complete stranger!" were the first words out of her mouth.

I explained to her why I was calling, filled her in on all the quirky coincidences leading up to that point, and asked if she'd be open to my coming by some afternoon to share some music. Dana was reluctant… to say the least.

"Umm… As long as you don't mind that my husband, four kids and two dogs will be there while we work."

I didn't buy into that "husband and kids" routine one bit. And, frankly, I didn't feel like dealing with somebody so suspicious.

"That's okay, Dana," I said. "Listen, I understand. It's probably best to leave things be. I wish you great success with your career." I hung up with no intention of contacting her again.

But, for whatever reason, Dana called me back.

"I apologize, Gary," she said. "I'm a little nervous about inviting over someone I don't know. But since Sid has met you… How about Saturday afternoon?"

And that Saturday in the spring of 1986, I showed

up at Dana's Manhattan apartment… wearing a Zorro mask and dragging a ball and chain on my leg! Sick, I know, but thankfully, Dana opened the door and took my lame attempt at humor in just the right spirit. We spent the rest of the day listening to each other's music and enjoying each other's company. I'll never forget how Dana walked me to the bus stop, and as I was about to leave, she said, "I don't know why, but I have a feeling we're going to do something special together." And when I got home to my apartment and my roomie, Mike Katzke, asked me how things went, I remember my exact reply: "This one could be special, Katzke."

And here we are today… Dana and I will soon celebrate our twenty-fifth wedding anniversary! We've written a ton of songs together in that time. Although several have been recorded by other artists, none have become radio hits. But when two soul mates find each other, as Dana and I did that April day in 1986? Well, somehow they know in their hearts that *their* hit song of all time is already in the process of being written.

Dana never erased that first phone message I left on her answering machine over a quarter-century ago. We still have a copy of that recording as well as the other videotapes of Dana's appearances on that Sid Bernstein show. Sid passed away a couple of years back at age ninety-five. To the rest of the world, he will be best remembered for introducing The Beatles to America. But, in my mind, he will always be the man who introduced my sweetheart to me. And for that, I will be eternally grateful.

— Gary Stein —

Meet Our Contributors

Vanessa Angone-Pompa received her MFA in Creative Writing from Columbia College Chicago in 2005. She is currently submitting the manuscript for her first novel for representation in hopes of publication. She enjoys writing, reading, traveling, and watching films. She and her husband are expecting their first child.

Sue Bonebrake received her BSE and MA from Northwest Missouri State University in 1969 and taught secondary and college English/Speech/Drama for almost thirty years. She and her husband have three children and three grandchildren. They have now retired and raise alpacas on a small acreage in northeast Iowa.

Denise Del Bianco is a retired widow living in her hometown—Bischwiller, France—after traveling the world with the love of her life, Pietro. After meeting in France, he and Denise raised two children in Italy and Canada. She enjoys cooking, reading and cuddling her furry grandkids. Her twitter handle is @DeniseBecht1.

Darla S. Grieco, M.S.Ed, is married with four children and resides near Pittsburgh, PA. In recent years she began writing, and is proud to be publishing her third story in the *Chicken Soup for the Soul* series. She has also been published in Guideposts' *Angels on Earth* magazine and shares lessons God has taught her at dsgrieco.com.

Louetta Jensen has written four mystery novels,

three screenplays and numerous short stories, most of which have garnered national and international awards.

Hugh Kent is a librarian who lives in Southern Ontario, Canada. He will be returning to China this summer to show his children the place where he met their mother.

JoAnne Macco worked for thirty years as a mental health therapist in a nonprofit agency. Since retiring, she paints angels, volunteers with first graders, and has published her first book, *Trust the Timing: A Memoir of Finding Love Again*. JoAnne lives in North Carolina with her husband, David, and their two dogs.

Jaymin J. Patel is the founder of www.JayminSpeaks. com. He travels around the world with his wife and two children helping people find wild success in their careers through his books, coaching, workshops, keynotes, and TEDx talk. He is grateful to his wife Eri for helping create this epic love story!

Gary Stein co-founded an NYSE-member investment banking firm. He was a strategy advisor to Lionsgate, Miramax and Seventh Generation and built a thirty-time Emmy-winning kids TV business. Gary is a proud mentor to several outstanding young women, and has been a frequent contributor to the *Chicken Soup for the Soul* series. E-mail him at gm.stein@verizon.net.

Meet
Amy Newmark

Amy Newmark is the bestselling author, editor-in-chief, and publisher of the *Chicken Soup for the Soul* book series. Since 2008, she has published 150 new books, most of them national bestsellers in the U.S. and Canada, more than doubling the number of Chicken Soup for the Soul titles in print today. She is also the author of *Simply Happy*, a crash course in Chicken Soup for the Soul advice and wisdom that is filled with easy-to-implement, practical tips for having a better life.

Amy is credited with revitalizing the Chicken Soup for the Soul brand, which has been a publishing industry phenomenon since the first book came out in 1993. By compiling inspirational and aspirational true stories curated from ordinary people who have had extraordinary experiences, Amy has kept the twenty-four-year-old Chicken Soup for the Soul brand fresh and relevant.

Amy graduated *magna cum laude* from Harvard University where she majored in Portuguese and minored in French. She then embarked on a three-decade career as a Wall Street analyst, a hedge fund manager, and a corporate executive in the technology field. She is a Chartered Financial Analyst.

Her return to literary pursuits was inevitable, as her honors thesis in college involved traveling throughout Brazil's impoverished northeast region, collecting stories from regular people. She is delighted to have come full circle in her writing career — from collecting stories "from the people" in Brazil as a twenty-year-old to, three decades later, collecting stories "from the people" for Chicken Soup for the Soul.

When Amy and her husband Bill, the CEO of Chicken Soup for the Soul, are not working, they are visiting their four grown children and their first grandchild.

Follow Amy on Twitter @amynewmark. Listen to her free podcast — "Chicken Soup for the Soul with Amy Newmark" — on Apple Podcasts, Google Play, the Podcasts app on iPhone, or by using your favorite podcast app on other devices.

Changing lives one story at a time®
www.chickensoup.com